Investing

Beginners Guide to Help Grow Your Money

Investing

© Copyright 2016 by J.J Potter - All rights reserved.

This document is geared towards providing exact and reliable information in regards to the topic and issue covered. The publication is sold with the idea that the publisher is not required to render accounting, officially permitted, or otherwise, qualified services. If advice is necessary, legal or professional, a practiced individual in the profession should be ordered.

- From a Declaration of Principles which was accepted and approved equally by a Committee of the American Bar Association and a Committee of Publishers and Associations.

In no way is it legal to reproduce, duplicate, or transmit any part of this document in either electronic means or in printed format. Recording of this publication is strictly prohibited and any storage of this document is not allowed unless with written permission from the publisher. All rights reserved.

The information provided herein is stated to be truthful and consistent, in that any liability, in terms of inattention or otherwise, by any usage or abuse of any policies, processes, or directions contained within is the solitary and utter responsibility of the recipient reader. Under no circumstances will any legal responsibility or blame be held against the publisher for any reparation,

Investing

damages, or monetary loss due to the information herein, either directly or indirectly.

Respective authors own all copyrights not held by the publisher.

The information herein is offered for informational purposes solely, and is universal as so. The presentation of the information is without contract or any type of guarantee assurance.

The trademarks that are used are without any consent, and the publication of the trademark is without permission or backing by the trademark owner. All trademarks and brands within this book are for clarifying purposes only and are the owned by the owners themselves, not affiliated with this document.

Investing

Table of Contents

Introduction	v
Chapter 1: What It Means To Invest	1
Chapter 2: Investments That Can Grow Your Money	6
Chapter 3: How To Decimate Your Fear Of Investing	12
Chapter 4: The Safety Of Investing In Mutual Funds	15
Chapter 5: Factors To Consider In Mutual Fund Investment	18
Conclusion	21
Chapter 4: Objection Handling	23

Investing

Introduction

I want to thank you and congratulate you for purchasing this book, *"Investing: Beginners Guide to Help Grow Your Money"*.

This book contains proven steps and strategies on how to invest your money. A good many people think that investing is a form of lifestyle meant for a particular category of rich guys. This book is going to show you otherwise. It is going to give you plain facts about investing, show you what investment entails and what good it brings you, and demonstrate how to go about the investment process. You will also learn what the repercussions of not investing are as well as the impact of investing poorly.

Is investing a dangerous undertaking? This question is going to be answered right here, and you will be able to see that there are many people growing their money the easy way only because they have understood how to minimize the risks associated with investment. You will learn what those safe investment techniques are and how you can best handle them. Growing your money need not remain a pipe dream. After reading through this book, you will see how achievable it is, whatever the size of your wallet.

Thanks again for purchasing this book, I hope you enjoy it!

Investing

Chapter 1: What It Means To Invest

Investing is simply putting some money aside so that it can produce some reward as time goes by. The reward you get from investing your money comes in different forms depending on where you have put the money, but the aspect that all forms of investing have in common is that of making you better off than you were before. If you have chosen to invest in business, you stand to reap profits; if it is in company debentures, which is a way of loaning money to a company, you are bound to earn interest; and if it is in stocks you stand to earn dividends. Even then, the rewards we have just mentioned are not exhaustive. Your capital, or the money you initially put in as investment, will still be growing. One of the greatest ways your investment grows when you put the money in business is accumulating goodwill. You can find your business goodwill growing from zero to tens of thousands of dollars within just a couple of years.

Any idea what goodwill is? Well, it is that positive outlook that people have towards your business, which would make you get business offers beyond what the business is really worth at market rate if you were to sell it as a going concern. Going what…? Yes, if you sell your business as it is so that the next businessperson takes it over and continues trading without much interruption, it is said you

Investing

are selling the business as a going concern. This is in contrast to times when you terminate your business by selling the individual assets and letting someone else lease out the empty premises.

Probably you took up a new building in a rather quiet neighborhood when you began your business, and now the place is buzzing with life because of the many customers that frequent your business. That means someone else can initiate another type of business in the area and take advantage of the people showing up because of you. Are you friendly with people? That also adds to your business goodwill. If people love you for your friendliness they will be willing to abandon other outlets just to visit yours. Has the area ceased to be lonely, courtesy of your business? That and all the other positive factors that can be linked to your business help to raise the value of your business in a big way, yet a way that cannot be explained step by step. Still, even with the complexity of explaining the build up to your goodwill, it is still an asset that is quantified monetarily. You will, in fact, find goodwill listed as an asset in the balance sheet of a business. It is an intangible asset.

When it comes to investing in stocks, your investment grows in value so that if today you sold part of the stocks you purchased five years ago, you would end up earning more money than you put in for those stocks that many years ago. That is generally what investment is about. As you can see, investing is a step further from saving because

Investing

when you save money, you mostly do not have it increasing in value; rather, you only keep it someplace safe.

How, then, can someone invest?

Investing is not rocket science. It is something that people have been doing for many years and are still doing it. So can we then term it a matter of common sense? No, we cannot. Many people keep dropping investment related terms in a way that can lead you to believe they are experts in investment matters even when they actually know very little. Reading books such as this one is the best way to equip you with worthwhile facts, something that will help you make wise investment decisions. Have you, for instance, had occasion to hear people talk of an ongoing IPO and how they would have gone for it if they had cash? Often a good number of those people cannot tell you anything else beyond the fact that the IPO is associated with such and such a company. Many may not even have an idea how the company has been doing for the past couple of years, let alone why the company has found it fit to issue an IPO at the time.

By the way, is the meaning of IPO obvious? IPO, in the field of investment, stands for *Initial Public Offer*. This means the company has been allowed to sell stocks to the public for the first time on the stock exchange. After the sale of those first stocks to the public, the company can no longer pass as a private entity. It straightaway becomes a

Investing

public company. This means its books of accounts will henceforth be open to public scrutiny, and office bearers will equally be answerable to the many members of the public who are now shareholders.

Anyway, the long and short of it is that although it is not difficult to invest, it is worth learning the options available in the market and the benefits and downside of each of them. Only then can you be in a position to choose the investment option that best suits you, your needs and your situation. For example, if you have an annual income of $10,000, just like your colleague in the office, but you have a family of five and he a family of three, you may, just like him, need to save and invest some money to beef up the company supported retirement package. However, can you afford to save and invest as much as your colleague? Probably no, considering the domestic bills you have to foot every month, which mostly correspond to the size of your family. But then again, you may, if you have kept your recurrent expenses low by living in a suburb that is less expensive than your colleague's residential area. This is how you evaluate your situation.

Are you willing to have a business running even as you continue working in the office? Probably your colleague does it, but if you were not born to juggle such serious commitments, you may end up messing up your performance in the office while doing a poor job of managing your business. Clearly, you may have similar needs as someone else and equal income as well, but other

Investing

factors come into play when choosing the type of investment that suits you; factors such as your personality and your circumstances.

Investing

Chapter 2: Investments That Can Grow Your Money

Are you willing to save some money for investment so that your money can grow? The greatest motivation when it comes to saving for investment is having a goal. When you have established what you want to do with your money after your investment has matured, you are likely to view the saving more positively rather than something that curtails your joy of spending. If your goal is to invest and use the money later on when you retire, you will be willing to spare the much that will help support your style of living when your regular income has stopped flowing in. If the goal is to accumulate enough money to travel the world in five years' time, similarly that goal will motivate you to save the much that will enable you to have fun in your travel.

If you want to reap optimum benefits, you need to settle on your goal or goals first. The next decision in line is where to invest the savings that you voluntarily set aside. Surely you cannot invest your savings in treasury bills if your goal is to build a retirement fund. Treasury bills pay up after a couple of months, so it would be ridiculous to put your money in them for retirement purposes. The reason some people make awkward investment decisions is really lack of information. You need to know the various investment options available and how they work, and then do an evaluation to see where you suit best.

Investing

Below Are Different Invest Categories

Assets

What would you say an asset is? Something that has value, probably...? So, when you invest in an asset, you are trying to grow your money by owning something of value. Hopefully, the value of your asset will increase over time, and you can look back and say you invested wisely. In investing, you want to own assets that you can convert into cash when it is time to implement your goal. When you own real estate property, this is an asset you have. When you buy securities such as company stocks or bonds, those are assets as well. And there are more.

Here are some terms you are going to hear often when discussing assets:

1) Holdings

   These refer to the specific assets that you hold or have, which may include stocks, bonds, debentures and more. They are actually the items that constitute your own investment portfolio. So, what would you say an investment portfolio is?

2) Portfolio

   If all your assets make up your portfolio, then it means your portfolio is your entire range of investments. Simply put, your investment portfolio

Investing

is the make-up of your assets in assembled form. Once in a while you are going to hear someone suggest that you expand your portfolio, and the meaning of that is simply that you need to invest in a different kind of asset as an addition to the assets you already have.

3) *Asset classes*

The general meaning of class is items that have similarities. In this case, asset classes refer to a set of assets that are similar in characteristics. For example, what would you say are the similarities between common stocks and preferred stocks? At a glance, you can recognize them as equity.

Sometimes, instead of speaking of assets in general, you find the assets being categorized variously as those that you own, those that you have lent out, and those that are liquid. Let us continue to review them here below:

1. *Investments that you own*

The reason you want to own an asset is so that you can dispose of it at a later date and in return get an amount of money in excess of the much you spent acquiring that asset. You can own lots of assets in this regard, but some of the most common ones are listed below:

a) Stocks

When you hear stocks in investment, think shareholding; think equity. The minute you

Investing

purchase stocks, you effectively become part of the company, owning membership. So, you do not just sit and wait for the stock prices to go up, you begin and continue to partake of dividends as the company reaps profits.

b)   Real Estate

The asset that falls under this category is that one which you purchase for the purposes of renting out or with the intention of re-selling it. Does that mean when you live in your house that building does not fall under real estate? Yes, it means exactly that. You cannot go saying that everyone in your area is in real estate investment only because they own the houses they live in. And the reason is simple – your living house is fulfilling a need that you cannot ignore even if you wanted to; a basic need. However, your rental house is generating income for you, and if you ever want to sell it, you are, very likely, going to fetch a sum of money in excess of its purchase price.

c)   Precious items

This category of assets includes items made of precious metal such as gold bracelets and diamond rings; precious art such as pieces from Da Vinci and Pablo Picasso's paintings; valuable souvenirs and collectibles; and others like those. When you have acquired such valuable items, you are almost certain that their value is increasing by the day and one day you could reap from them multi-fold.

Investing

d) Business

Once you have invested in a business, it means you own something that is increasing your money. That is why your business is categorized as an investment that you own.

2. *Investments created out of lending*

These are investments that are made in form of debt. What you do is lend the company money, but instead of being referred to as a creditor like the suppliers who lend the company goods to use in the business, you are considered a buyer of sorts. And what is it will you be buying? The answer is debt. You will understand it better when we describe the various investments that fall under this category.

a) Bonds

Often the term bond is used to refer to any instrument that you purchase to show the company owes you the equivalent of its value. So if you purchase 8% 5yr government bonds worth $10,000, you are going to receive exactly $10,000 at the end of the 5yr period. Then why bother investing in bonds? Well, the company will not have traded with your money for nothing. They will have paid you interest at the rate of 8% p.a.

b) Certificate of Deposit or CDs

These ones are more like bonds, only that they are issued by banks. With the CDs, you are essentially lending money to the bank by purchasing these instruments that are a form of IOU. What you do is actually save money with the bank the way you would in a savings account, only this time you do not withdraw bits of that money as you wish. Once you have received a CD, it is tantamount to lending the bank money for a predetermined length of time. You can actually look at it as allowing the bank to hold your savings in a fixed account for a period you and the bank agree upon. CDs, like bonds, earn you interest. Does your savings account not attract interest? Well, any interest earned in a savings account is usually peanuts. On the contrary, buying CDs is real investment and the bank offers a more favorable rate of interest.

3. *Investments that are cash equivalent*

   These are investments that you can quickly turn into cash. A good example is cash held in a commercial bank's savings account.

One thing you need to realize is that the investments whose returns are guaranteed such as bonds, CDs and savings accounts have low yields compared to those whose yields fluctuate according to market forces. Do you know the reason? It is because for the ones with unpredictable returns, such as stocks, the risk is, obviously, higher. The principle in investment is the higher the risk the higher the yield and vice-versa.

Investing

Chapter 3: How to Decimate Your Fear of Investing

Are you afraid of losing money? Who really isn't? But then again, some people are more fearful than others. And also as in all other endeavors, you must risk something to gain something. In sports, you risk hurting your body, yet you exercise, practice and prepare and hope to win a medal or at least make the cut for the next tournament. In acting, you sometimes risk making a fool of yourself, yet you take up the challenge hoping you could win a Grammy or such other reward. And so is it with investing. There is always some degree of risk whenever you put out some of your money for investment, and so it is understandable that you should have some fear over it.

Main reasons why some people are afraid of investing:

1. They are worried they might lose their money

2. They have no inkling how to choose the appropriate time to invest

3. Market volatility scares them stiff

4. They have no idea there is something like an investment portfolio, and when they know it, they do not know how to manage it.

5. They fret that some need may arise where cash is needed fast and they do not have it because they have put it into investment

Investing

All these reasons make an understandable basis for fear. However, the thought of investors like Warren Buffett, who have gotten wealthy through investing, should make you realize that the risk involved in investment is worth it, particularly when well calculated. That's it – calculation! You can use the fear that you have as motivation to critically evaluate the investments at your disposal, thus helping you to make the best investment decisions possible.

In short, fear of failing to grow your money as hoped need not stop you from investing. Once you learn the details about investing, you are going to see that you can have different types of investments, so that as you lose a percentage point here, you probably gain three percentage points on another investment. As such, your net yield becomes the plus you have been hoping for – overall growth of your investments.

How to Overcome Your Fear of Investing

a)   Learn some basic finance and investment principles

Ideally, it would be recommended that you take up some finance and investment course, but is time always on your side? Something you can do from the comfort of your home or office is reading material such as that contained in this book, so that you can furnish yourself with the fundamental principles of investing. You may also wish to listen to podcasts prepared by investment gurus, as they often decipher myths associated with investment in a way you can easily understand.

b)   Be ready to diversify

Investing

Try and avoid the temptation to get glued to a single investment no matter how attractive it may look today. Remember we spoke of risks? Who knows how the market will be months or years down the line for that particular investment? But my capital outlay is small... Worry not – there are investment funds that take what you call small investment capital and manage to spread it over different assets, so that your money is invested in assets with varying levels of risk.

c)   *Invest reasonably long-term*

Of course it is understandable you may not want to hold all your investment money for decades, but do try to let it lie for at least 5yrs. Even with the volatility that prevails in the investment market, the ups and downs that happen over years usually evens out. So you are unlikely to liquidate your investment at a lower value than it was when you invested in it. On the contrary, you could lose big by liquidating your investment in panic only weeks or months after stock prices begin falling.

Investing

Chapter 4: The Safety of Investing In Mutual Funds

Is a mutual fund an investment? Well, it is not exactly an investment the way you would view stocks or bonds – no. It is a fund. You, I and some other people put some money into the fund, and so we, kind of, own the fund mutually. The officers, who manage the fund then take the money pooled in the fund, and with the help of experts, decide on the best investments to buy for the people who have bought into the fund. Mutual funds are able to collect large sums of money, and so they are able to buy a wide range of investments. They can invest in high yield stocks even when they carry a high risk, and at the same time invest in government bonds which normally provide low yields, but which are almost risk free. This is the kind of diversity you have seen recommended in the earlier chapter.

It is unlikely that all types of investments can lose market value at the same time. If you look at the case of China, there are times the manufacturing sector suffers and so stocks in the manufacturing companies drop in value, but it happens to be the same time that trading companies are smiling all the way to the bank. So as the steel industry, for example, suffers, companies trading in consumable goods are flourishing and their stocks are rising in value. If your investment portfolio has investments from both sectors, as you can see, you cannot entirely lose. By virtue of being a shareholder in a mutual fund, you are by extension an investor with a diversified portfolio.

Let it be said here also that sometimes individual mutual funds choose to confine themselves in a particular type of investment. In such cases, even when they diversify, they do so within their chosen investment category. If, for instance, a mutual fund invests in fixed income investments, their portfolio may comprise government and company bonds, treasury bills, and even CDs. Of course there are those funds that invest liberally and you need to get the facts right before making your decision on the kind of fund you want to invest in. You also have a choice to create your own portfolio of mutual funds; meaning you could invest in different kinds of mutual funds. That spreads your risk even further, effectively minimizing it.

Here are some types of existing mutual funds you could choose from:

1. *The Money Market Mutual Funds*

    These ones deal with fixed income, low risk securities, mostly from the government and blue chip companies. Their investments include bonds, treasury bills and even debentures. That list is by any count exhaustive.

2. *Stocks Mutual Funds*

    If there are mutual funds that can afford to pay you high yields, these are it. You could have a year when the value of your stocks skyrockets and you can see yourself becoming a millionaire. By the same token, you could have such a bad year that you almost regret why you invested in the particular mutual fund. The reality is that stock prices fluctuate at will, because they are influenced by many factors, including the weather and politics. Still, remember your mutual fund may have investments in different sectors, ranging from manufacturing to trading, and tourism and hospitality in between. So, you are not entirely exposed in a mutual fund.

3. *Hybrid Funds*

Investing

If you are not so much averse to risk and again not too liberal in matters of investment, this may just be the mutual fund for you. It combines what number one and two above do. They buy high risk but high yield stocks; invest in the fixed and relatively low yield but low risk securities such as bonds; and of course, they do not hesitate to try out whatever other investment is in the market if they deem it fit.

Do you now see why you may consider mutual funds relatively safe to invest in? You can go fully conservative and be content with yields that are equally conservative, or you can invest in a mutual fund dealing with high risk stocks, but stand a chance to reap multi-fold, with the consolation that the stocks may not necessarily be in the same sector. Then you have the option of investing in the fund that is not very selective, and have your risk spread over different investment types and sectors, and stand to reap yields that are impressive while not necessarily mind boggling.

Investing

Chapter 5: Factors to consider in Mutual Fund Investment

The renowned American economist with British roots, Benjamin Graham, is reported to have termed an intelligent investor as one who does research on various assets with a view to investing in the most promising ones, as opposed to entrusting the work to someone else. While you may have good reasons of engaging a financial advisor to do the necessary due diligence, you need to realize that there is an important factor that influences investment decisions, which the expert may not know – your personality. Of course, if you choose to invest in a mutual fund you are going to enjoy the services from experts by virtue of being a member of the fund, but here your personality does not matter much as the investment risk is absorbed and minimized by the great variety of investments involved.

Still, you just cannot reap yields without a bit of intelligent thinking. As such, you need to know the factors to weigh, to help you make up your mind when it is that investing in a mutual fund is best for you.

   (1) *How the fund has been doing in recent years?*

> The point here is that it is not easy to make reasonable judgment regarding the performance of a fund by watching the share performance over weeks, months or even a year. You can only tell if the mutual fund has a skilled and diligent manager who is influencing performance by observing the share performance over a period of say, three to five years. In the short term, as Benjamin Graham says, the fluctuations are mostly random.

Investing

(2) *Due diligence performance*

This is a factor you cannot afford to ignore even when you are planning to invest through a mutual fund. Some background check on the individuals who make up the fund's management team can do you some good. If, for instance, you find names of individuals who have been in management teams whose companies or funds failed under their watch, you do not want to join potential victims.

It is also a good time to establish how the mutual fund organizes its asset allocation. Now that you know what types of assets are highly risky and which ones are relatively safe, you can tell when the fund's portfolio is too lopsided for you. Without doing due diligence, you could find yourself buying into a fund that is skewed towards stocks and yet your personality is somewhat conservative. That is how some people end up investing in a fund and asking to sell their shares in just a couple of months, after they somehow discover it was not the fund them.

As many experts and experienced investors will tell you, buying an investment today and selling it before the dust has settled is ill advised. That mode of operation does not accomplish what investing is meant to do – make your money grow. Instead, you end up making losses from frequent transaction costs and other details.

(3) *The fee issue*

Why would you commit your money into a mutual fund before knowing the amount of fees it charges to transact and before gauging that against what other mutual funds charge? Some funds charge such high fees that even when they return high yields, you cannot see that in positive light as most of your gains will have been eaten up by transaction and other incidental costs.

(4) Weighing the fund against other investment options

When you want to make some savings and you do not want to risk your money losing value because of inflation, a mutual fund may be your best option. This is particularly so if the other investments available in the market at the time are all high risk. The only decision you would need to make in such circumstances is the kind of mutual fund you want – money market based, stock based or hybrid.

On the overall, investing in mutual funds is advisable, because everything considered, you would be better off investing through an entity that has the benefit of expert advice from finance and investment advisors, than go it alone when you are not well versed with the intricacies of the investment market. Also as a new investor, your money can grow reasonably well and you still feel cushioned from possible investment losses, the kind that individual stocks are susceptible to.

Conclusion

Thank you again for purchasing this book!

I hope this book was able to help you to appreciate the goodness that comes with investing. It is also my hope that you have enjoyed reading the book and grasped the basics of investment. Hopefully, I have managed to allay any fears you may have had regarding putting your money into investments, and instead got you interested and enthusiastic about growing your money.

After going through the simplified information provided in this book, you must have realized that not all types of investments are risky. You must also have learnt that even for the relatively risky investments, there is a way of shielding yourself from potential losses, even as you stand a chance to multiply your money over time. With the information still fresh in your mind, it may be the right time to think about investing to grow your money. If you are already into some investment, you may wish to use your newly acquired knowledge to either build an investment portfolio, or to expand your existing one.

The next step is to use the knowledge you have acquired here to help you take advantage of prevailing market opportunities and prepare for a brighter and richer future.

Investing

Finally, if you enjoyed this book, then I'd like to ask you for a favor. Would you be kind enough to leave a review for this book on Amazon? It'd be greatly appreciated!

Click here to leave a review for this book on Amazon!

Thank you and good luck!

Investing

Preview of 'Sales: Techniques to Increase and Close Sales Faster"

Chapter 4: Objection Handling

Objection management is part and parcel of any sales process. Objections rear their seemingly ugly heads right from the first time you meet a client and at times many continue to torment you even after the product is sold. For a good sales person, objections are seen not as obstacles but as business opportunities. If a customer is spending time to illustrate an objection, then it means your customer is an interested party and the chances of a closed sale are high.

Objections, broadly, are divided into a few strategic categories and some of them are:
- I am happy with a similar product from your competitor
- Send me information on mail and I will revert to you
- I am not at all interested. Do not bother me
- I need this but right now it is not a priority
- Your pricing is high

Irrespective of what the objections are, remember the following points in managing and handling them:

Prepare yourself for the objections – Make copious notes, create virtual solutions, brainstorm with colleagues and do everything that is needed to

Investing

ensure that you have answers to most of the expected objections of your product(s). For this, you need to know your products inside-out. Practice your answer preferably with a colleague. Do not make calls without knowing your products really well. This will ensure that, more often not, you are ready with an emphatic answer for most of the questions.

Show gratitude for the objection raised by the customer – Always thank the customer first when he raises an objection. You must remember that objections are pathways to a successful deal closure and gratitude for such opportunities must be exhibited.

Empathize with your customer – When you empathize with your customer you connect at a very personal level. Listen intently and show that you understand and care for his comments and objections. Use "I'm sorry you feel like that," "I understand your frustration," "I know how you feel but I think I can help you with that," and more such empathizing language. Beware of getting defensive about your product; this attitude will only enhance the divide between you and your customer.

Now get down to brass tacks – once the emotional angle has been managed, you can work towards the details of the objections and here is where your preparing sessions will come in extremely handy. Rephrase the same question so that you get answers that tell exactly what objections and issues the customer has. Remember to build a good rapport during the discussion phase. Do not convert it into an argumentative process wherein you are trying to prove yourself right.

Remember you do not need to be right; you just need to close the deal for yourself.

Emphasize the value in your products – For sustained customer loyalty, remember to show them what value your products deliver. The process of customer discovery includes knowing what he needs from your product and how you can present it in a way that he relates to. Use various irrefutable proofs to emphasize the value in your product.

A few effective answers for common objections:

I am happy with a similar product from your competitor – Respond by focusing on the unique aspects of your product and other value-added services not included in the competitor's product.

Send me information on email and I will revert to you – While you confirm/ask for the correct email ID, give specific options including day and time. Or ask which days and/or times are convenient for him. These questions will ensure that the lead remains active and you can follow up later.

I am not interested at all; do not bother me – These clear-cut shutdown statements require experienced handling skills. You have to probe gently and find out what your customer's real interests are and then take it forward. Let the customer see your genuine curiosity and concern when he opens up with further objections.

Pricing – This is possibly the most basic and unavoidable objection of any sale. There are research reports that reveal most price objections are phony meaning to say the customer is not interested in the pricing as much as he is interested

Investing

in knowing what exactly he is saving through your product. Be ready with answers! As these questions are expected you can easily prepare for them and handle them such that pricing issue never comes back during any discussion.

Like most difficult things in the world, managing objections requires patience and plenty of practice. You will see your confidence and capabilities increasing with every call and customer interaction. Your seniors and your colleagues are your support system. Leverage the experiences of your seniors and share learning experiences with your colleagues and see yourself becoming a pro sooner than later.

Always present your product in the way your customer wants to see it and not necessarily in the way you see it. Be patient with your customer; build a good rapport with him; discover his needs; all these will make you an effective salesperson and your customer's loyalty will be assured.

Check Out My Other Books

Below you'll find some of my other popular books that are popular on Amazon and Kindle as well. Simply click on the links below to check them out. Alternatively, you can visit my author page on Amazon to see other work done by me.

Sales: Techniques to Increase and Close Sales Faster

www.ingramcontent.com/pod-product-compliance
Lightning Source LLC
Chambersburg PA
CBHW070428190526
45169CB00003B/1453